A LITTLE BLACK BOOK
OF POETRY

A LITTLE BLACK BOOK OF POETRY

by
JOHNATHON SIERING

RESOURCE *Publications* • Eugene, Oregon

A LITTLE BLACK BOOK OF POETRY

Resource Publications
An Imprint of Wipf and Stock Publishers
199 W. 8th Ave., Suite 3
Eugene, OR 97401

www.wipfandstock.com

PAPERBACK ISBN: 979-8-3852-0076-4
HARDCOVER ISBN: 979-8-3852-0077-1
EBOOK ISBN: 979-8-3852-0078-8

VERSION NUMBER 01/04/24

CONTENTS

WEEKDAY WEEKENDS

Walk early morning streets
fog-rain covered in sunlight streaks,

I'll saunter to a low-key café
wantin' a sip of morning-problem-away,

I'll watch the hustle-n-bustle of kids and adults
dropped at school, then off to the work waltz.

That'll help lay way to a lazy afternoon
in page after page turning me a reading buffoon,

then the next biggest thing is
What's For Lunch: A Pop Quiz;

That will be poolside with cheese
and charcuteries,

drinkin' on a smooth
20s Sci-Fi while sippin a bourbon-n-sweet tea to soothe

time before dinner. Then perhaps I'll play on my knees,
or a foot race, catch-chase, tug-o-war with the dog like a pagan
worship on battle's eve,

and when it gets late and way after pets are fed
I'll stroll through moonlight to a wanting bed

to lay in wait for what dreams might come
of love, adventure, or pointed at me a loaded gun,

possibly of falling, swimming, strolling through a park
where I take a balloon to get anchovy ice cream with Frank, a
friendly shark.

But those are uncivilized dreams
shuddering as I think to myself while a blazon sun set beams;

Either way tomorrow's a non-workday
I get to do it again, but in a different way.

HERE ARE A FEW OF MY FAVORITE THINGS

Droplets on tushies and whiskey on whiskers,
All colored titties and explicit pictures,
UPS packages left out just for me,
Here are a few of my favorite things.

Podcasts that's senseless or TV broadcasting,
Dragons that stop black-arcana from casting,
Watching a live stream of a criminal spree,
Here are a few of my favorite things.

Half work day, short work day, no work day glory
Telling a bad joke that's inflammatory
Eating of cheese and fine charcuteries
Here are a few of my favorite things.

When they box fight,
When the cake's baked
When I'm feeling mad
I simply remember my favorite things
And then I do feel . . .   so glad.

"ELEPHANT SEALS AND LIGHTHOUSES"—A PHOTO BY JONATHON CROCKETT POSTED ON FACEBOOK

Here in Morro Bay
Here in Morro Bay
Animals and shrubberies live and play
Animals and shrubberies live and play
Here bay animals play and . . .
and in Morrow shrubberies live

Sandy slope leads to a sandy beach,
Sandy slope leads to a sandy beach,
Elephant seals sleep soundly
Elephant seals sleep soundly
Sandy beach slope leads to sandy
Elephant seals soundly a sleep

Lighthouse warns with light and horn,
Lighthouse warns with light and horn,
While waves crash on rocks the sea adorns
While waves crash on rocks the sea adorns
Light and horn adorns rocks on the sea;
With waves crash while lighthouse warns

A Lighthouse warns
in light and with horn;
Sandy shrubberies live and sandy animals play,
slope here leads to Morro Bay,
soundly waves crash, and the sea adorns beach rocks,
elephant seals sleep on.

A SPIDER'S SECRET

I wait and wait
and I wait some more
with a bait
on my breath close to the floor.

I wait all day,
perhaps a week
or more, only to hear you say
"Look at this freak

who crawls on the floor." I run, click-clack-click-clack-click-clack
as I'm off
to get a snack.
Please don't scoff,

and do not spew
for I'm just a spider in tap shoes.

A BALLY TABLE KING

Let loose the silver ball
Let loose the silver ball
Light flashes while bells ring
Light flashes while bells ring
While ball loose; ring silver bells
Light let flashes

Flap your flippers, make aim right
Flap your flippers, make aim right
Accumulate more points from multi-ball holes
Accumulate more points from multi-ball holes
more your flippers flap make multi-ball holes, aim right,
points accumulate

I hope to beat an Electronic Bally Table King
I hope to beat an Electronic Bally Table King
To leave my name on a random tiny screen
To leave my name on a random tiny screen
Bally Table King on a random tiny screen; I,
My name to leave, an tiny electronic hope to beat

A tiny electronic screen, random bell ring,
I to make more the light flashes,
Let loose your flippers flap
While silver ball accumulate points,
Aim right to be an Bally table King from multi-ball holes;
hope my name leave on . . .

A WITCH'S POT LUCK

I hear the happy cackles
of witches, three, gathered round
a silver modern-model cauldron, got not for free,

within which sits and simmers aromatic shackles
that fetter nostrils in glee upon sacred cooks ground
where shoulder, non-paldron, need to flee.

They let the brew blot and spot
air that's hot while wooden spoon circle-stirs
a chant starts up as juice is squeezed

"foil foil the meat we then broil
for the stove is on and pot does boil
with carrot, onion, and potato . . .

an wok we coat with oil,
pack-to-pack till pan turns throng . . .
pull out strong, then top with tomato . . .

now we add ear of corn
and eye of radish,
while slow we cook the head of cabbage . . . "

My demon of gluttony growels
and grows in this mobil vessel
now lead by nose;

then with eager tremblin jowls
the demon escapes within my howls
as the witches concoction entombs it in gruntled food satiation.

No scorn as we stand in line,
non-abbash for a second time
of more magically delicious adage
We start up a chant:

Double double the broil
meat and soup that bubble,
add filet of carrot,
extra slice of cake,
slather sauteed brussel
sprouts, and this salmon bake . . .

I'll finish this and so much more with vigorous hustle,
For at this witch's potluck I am no trouble.

PARADELLE FOR A FOREST

Look there beyond the hills above a foggy skyline
Look there beyond the hills above a foggy skyline
Survey a sleepy town square, just before sunrise
Survey a sleepy town square, just before sunrise
Beyond a sleepy town survey, look just before sunrise;
The hills, there above foggy skyline a square.

On mountain pass, smell of fresh pines,
On mountain pass, smell of fresh pines,
I remark about our hamlet below sullen skies
I remark about our hamlet below sullen skies
Our sullen hamlet, fresh skies pass about,
Smell the mountain of pines, I remark on. . .

Love the forest like a second home,
Love the forest like a second home,
All about it, I enjoy the roam.
All about it, I enjoy the roam.
A forest all about I like to roam;
Love it, enjoy the second home.

Look beyond the mountain of pines,
Survey below a sleepy foggy town skyline;
The square, a hamlet, a sullen smell,.
Hill Above fresh forest, our love, the second home,
I remark all about the roam,
I enjoy it.

DDONG CHIM

For those who know
my name, I lie in wait;
clearance for my cargo
seals your fate.

I'm always on the prowl
day or night,
wants to make you howl,
watch you take flight.

To summon me, my playing fans,
in a gun position
you'll put your hands;
that's the start of this friendly imposition;

Poke quick no hesitation,
at the bum, . . . no penetration.

A PARADELLE FOR A PARADELLE

I tend to repeat myself,
I tend to repeat myself,
What an echo with a changed voice
What an echo with a changed voice
With an echo I tend to what
Myself, a changed repeat voice.

Am the child of a poet laureate,
Am the child of a poet laureate,
Yet here I sit, virtually unknown.
Yet here I sit, virtually unknown.
Here I sit, child unknown, yet virtually of
The poet, a laureate

I end in an amalgamation,
I end in an amalgamation,
Again I begin from inspiration.
Again I begin from inspiration.
In amalgamation from an inspiration;
I begin . . . I end . . .again

Here I end; what am I,
Myself, with a changed voice, yet I repeat
In an echo amalgamation
Tend an inspiration, a child
Of a poet, virtually from the laureate
To sit unknown . . . begin again.

A POEM ABOUT A POEM, But It Has A Really Long Loquacious Title That Doesn't Say Anything Or Give Any Clues About The Poem Itself But Just Goes On And On About Nothing Until Most Of The Time That Has Been Taken Up By The Reader Was Done By Reading Just The Title, That Title That Is Just Now Being Read; But You The Reader, Could Have Finished The Poem Several Times Over, And Is Left Wondering Why I Would Do Such A Thing, To You Reader, As To Come Up With Such An Exhaustible Title For No Real Reason Other Than The One That I Am About To Tell You About And That Is, With The Simple Answer Being An Answer That You Do Really Want To Hear But Have Not Yet Because I'm Trying To Keep You Here Reading This Absurdity Of A Title For As Long As Possible, Which Is: Because I Can

This is my haiku:
It goes 5, 7, 5, and
now this is the end

PARADELLE FOR COMICS

I am limitless to the hoarder.
I am limitless to the hoarder.
We are fantastic to the fanatic.
We are fantastic to the fanatic.
To the fanatic hoarder we are to the
Limitless; I am, we are, fantastic

Action from cover to back page
Action from cover to back page
With it love somewhere in between
With it love somewhere in between
Action, with love from somewhere in
It, between cover to back page.

Children, adults, even moody teens
Children, adults, even moody teens
Enjoy the fables, not hard to gage
Enjoy the fables, not hard to gage
Not hard adults, to children,
Gage the moody teens - enjoy fables –

The fanatic action from moody teens,
Children to adults; limitless fantastic
Fables in between the cover to back page.
I am, we are, with the hoarder
Somewhere to hard to gage . . .
To not to Enjoy it . . . even love it . . .

GINGERBREAD FAMILY COMES FOR THE HOLIDAY

Gingerbread men,
and gingerbread kids,
with gingerbread women;
eating this gingerbread family, instructions forbids.

In a gingerbread house
on gingerbread lane
everything but a gingerbread mouse
propped up in the yard with a gingerbread cane.

They'll exist throughout the holiday
greeting the kids, taunting hungry dogs,
but I'll keeping mine up till May
just so they can hear croaking of frogs.

. . . never mind it's all fallen apart,
building this is for kids, and I'm an old fart.

WILMA RUDOLPH

Sprint, dash, run,
Sprint, dash, run
100 200 meters down; fun
100 200 meters down; fun
Dash 100, Sprint 200
Fun run down meters

Fast along Roman tracks you came
Fast along Roman tracks you came
3 golds in the 1960's game
3 golds in the 1960's game
Roman tracks, you fast, in the 1960's games
Along came 3 golds

You elevated track and field
You elevated track and field
A role model; Black athletes unconcealed
A role model; Black athletes unconcealed
Black athletes elevated track and field;
You a role model, unconcealed.

The Game: in 1960's Roman
Track and field 100, 200,
meters fun-dash-sprint-run.
Along fast track you came; 3 golds down,
A role model for athletes,
Black, you elevated unconcealed.

PLUMB GIN AND DANDELION WINE

Shady spot with book in hand,
relax pool-side,
wish it was sand;
at least I got blue sky-ed.

With chair set up,
feet stretched out,
plum gin in one hand . . . what,
the other? Dandelion Wine, I spout,

with over half the bottle done,
ditto on the book.
This day had its fun,
and I'm overcooked

from Dandelion Wine and plum gin,
so I sway away inside with a slurred grin.

SICK DAY TODAY

Slick streets
and runny noses
drops fast on feet
like connected to hoses;

Collected crumpled tissue
with nose offerings
off to one side next to the unwanted issue
of coffee rings.

A warning
call on the pending day break,
a not-so-good morning,
to which H.R. suspects a fake.

Either way comes unwanted urges;
no work due to projectile purges

T.P.'S EPITAPH

Etiolate our complexion, for
We care not;
When I'm no more
You'll be quite distraught.

Oh how I
love to roll on and on
getting used up, flushed down; bye-bye
shit pawns.

Easy find
cozy on shelves,
as my kind
arrives in sixes, eights, twelves.

My downfall is the bidet;
No hands, they say, is "the future way"

TOMES OF DELICIOUSNESS

What wise wizard of
Culinary capabilities used
this tome of food love;
Ancient sullied pages fused

with time poured
into every measurement, every word
with annotations left as a record
for adjustment of all items stirred.

Chapters and chapters of graciously gratifyingly gluttonous
gastronomies
Paired with succulently saucy spells,
To be enjoyed under heavenly astronomy
at the ringing of the dinner bell.

This can be all yours to master,
Just pick up any of these culinary codex, become a food caster.

TO COOK A COOKBOOK

To cook
a cook-book
in any kitchen,
which will smell of fresh herbs
and exotic spices,
you will need vegetable

slices. Lots and lots of vegetable
slices, some to cook
with fancy spices,
and others to be stewed with the cooking book
(probably called *Cooking in Herb's
Secret kitchen*).

Remember, no bitchin' in the kitchen
just vegetables,
herbs,
water to cook
Herb's soon to be cooked book,
and don't forget the spices.

Yes, add all the spices
we have in the kitchen
to the cooking book,
with the sliced vegetables
that we cut, to cook
with the herbs

that were suggested by Herb's,
now, delicious smelling spiced
infused book that we cook
in our super-secret kitchen,
with our home grown vegetables
we learned to grow from a gardening book.

A gardening book
Called: For growin' herbs,
vegetables,
and spices
that one would use in a kitchen
(with annotated instructions for fresh, dried, or pre-cook

foods). Though upon reflection I do not recommend that you
stew vegetables with a cookbook
or to even cook one, even with herbs
and spices, in any kitchen to make it taste good.

(SORCERY IN) LAUREL'S KITCHEN

What a wise wizard, master
of forgotten tomes
left by colloquial sorceress of
culinary disciplines.

Sift through the whole
codex of cuisine
for succulent spells to
delight, entertain,

soothe or pander for your Kings and Queens;
careful and take note
of inscribed annotations
-peel egg, remove onion skin-

Young witch darts
left   and   right in post haste as one who's
caught fright.
Hastily and methodically she applies her saucy art,
to chop ever faster as the spell's components

foam to life and hiss
angry at a famished caster,
unless caldron thee has drained;
Now transfer to bowl with more butter

for smells of deliciousness to waft through the air,
please take a gander
at this concoction with no meat,
a delicious stew-potion . . . and no salamander.

For this spell's power I will not keep with
wicked witch intentions for meat eaters with preconceived condition
here in Laurel's, smell binding, Kitchen
of vegetarian cookery and nutrition.

100 FAMOUS WOMEN

Rosa Luxemburg, Helen Keller, Jane Addams, Princess Diana, Wangari Maathai, Rosa Parks,

Emmeline Pankhurst, Margaret Sanger, Harriet Chalmers Adams, Mother Teresa, Lois Mailou Jones, Mary Higgins Clark, Lee Krasner, Georgia O'Keeffe, Harriet Quimby, Nadia Comaneci, Babe Didrikson Zaharias, Bonnie Blair, Althea Gibson, Steffi Graf, Oprah Winfrey,

Billie Jean King, Jackie Joyner-Kersee, Cher, Audrey Hepburn, Jacqueline Cochran,

Annie Oakley, Raymonde de Laroche, Amelia Earhart, Rachel Carson, Grandma Moses,

Sally Ride, Marie Curie, Elizabeth Arden, Coco Chanel, Hillary Clinton, Helena Rubinstein, Martha Stewart, Madame CJ Walker, Joan Baez, Dorothy Dandridge, Dorothy Hodgkin,

Jane Fonda, Martina Navratilova, Nancy Wake, Grace Kelly, Madonna, Susan Atkins,

Maya Angelou, Sonja Henie, Barbra Streisand, Bessie Coleman, Bette Davis, Edith Cavell,

Irena Sendler, Helen Thayer, Gloria Steinem, Mae Jemison, Valentina Tereshkova,

Gertrude Bell, Jane Goodall, Dian Fossey, Rosalind Franklin, Barbara McClintock, Margaret Mead, Typhoid Mary,

Marilyn Monroe, Griselda Blanco, Jeannette Rankin, Lisa Meitner, Eva Peron, Mata Hari,

Tokyo Rose, Ethel Rosenberg, Corazon Aquino, Benazir Bhutto, Shirley Chisolm,

Frances Perkins, Queen Elizabeth II, Indira Gandhi, Frida Kahlo, Sandra Day O'Connor,

Estee Lauder, Bonnie Parker, Eleanor Roosevelt, Ellen Johnson Sirleaf, Anne Frank

Aung San Suu Kyi, Golda Meir, Virginia Woolf , Agatha Christie, Lynette "Squeaky" Fromme, Aretha Franklin,Toni Morrison, Joyce Carol Oates, Alice Walker

J.K. Rowling, Anne Rice, Margaret Thatcher, Wilma Rudolp.

Josephine Baker (who wasn't left out).

These were the famous women of the 20th century,
Join their ranks, destroy the male built penitentiary.
I don't want to leave your name off,
Fight for better rights, maybe throw a Molotov*,
Study hard and drink from the suffrage trough,
Do and cook only what, when, where you want . . . maybe . . .
stroganoff?

*I do not condone the throwing of Molotov cocktails to achieve
equality.

A PERFECT DAY

It would probably
be on a Wednesday
with a slight chill,

and clouds
that sail low
and snail slow;

Some of them would be grays
others would be white,
speckles the sky even at night.

Spring would have been sprung
among green mountains where one can dally
within morning frost shadowed valleys,

The streets would be
quiet enough to hear
a cow's call or a horse's cheer,

but mostly you could just
lay in a warm cozy bed and not be bothered
while you sloth your way through this perfect day.

A WINTER MORNING

This time on my morning walk I watch
As the breeze plucks
perfect leaves

of oranges, crimsons, and hay colors
and drops them from
tree tops to head tops,

all the while it plays with the birds,
and the silver-gray clouds that linger low
slowly strolling above the town.

It tousles my hair,
gives me a brumal
hug that I do not decline, while I turn

my smile to scan upon the
Wester horizon knowing The Smell:
the ripeness of clouds that linger,

waiting,
wanting
to let loose their liquid life load upon the ground;

but my thoughts
turn to warm beds, pots
of hot chocolate and peppermint shots;

damn this perfect
weather ruined
by a work day.

DEATH DAY ANNIVERSARY

I took the day off,
I wanted to get lost
in remembrance of those whose mortal coils got cut off
too soon or at great cost.

I did little,
drank much;
It's fickle to pin down one tittle
memory to lighten my mood and such.

Memories of grandmothers, mothers,
neighbors, friends,
fathers and brothers;
hearts cry to cleanse.

This begs the questions of:
how many years left
before I get dirt above;
will I have my teeth, my eyes, or my ears be deft-ed?

Will there be revelry in my decay,
will I have company once
a month, a week, a day?
Will my marker be fancy, perhaps a dunce?

I haven't visited those,
in years,
who doze
beneath the earth in my future fears.

I want to be held,
I want to cry,

I want one more "I love you" yelled,
I want one more time to say goodbye.

COME WITH ME, YOU STRAY DOG

Good morning dog
You faithful hound
Breakfast time of some grog,
After we'll meander around.

Hello my propitious friend
New acquaintance of mine,
Who I've come to amend
The wrongs against descendants of lupine

Come with me, no need to fear,
I love you dog (under rusted car I peer),

Afternoon dog, you
Constant cur, you look hot
Come with me to find a new
Cooler spot.

Salutations my consort canine client,
Come with me home;
It's peaceful, silent.
It's where my love is sown.

Come with me, no need to fret,
I love you dog let me give you pets,

Evening dog, now trusted mutt,
You mangy mongrel,
Dinner's ready in the hut,
bar-b-que of the Mongols

Come with me, no need to for dread
I love you dog (on my knees I plead)

Oh, my forever puppy, you furry
Bundle of agape love
Who gives kisses of tongue flurries
When you tower above.

Come with me, you dastard bastard,
I love you dog, let me be your loving master.

DEATHBED

here I Am, laying
in a state of bed rest,
soon eternal rest, in this rest bed.

you come in and

                                               see me here

as you're used to these past two weeks,

waiting for my
end to this life,
suffering-joy-suffering-suffering-peace;

My death-rattle
shakes you from your
long   hum   song,

as touch is heightened, fear in your
hands, grips tighten,
straining ears for every last word

of whispered voice, all warm
Memories   Of   Us,
caresses this shaken heart,

as my lacrima mortis moves
on my cheek, now
here i am   released.

RANCH IN PACHECO'S PASS

Fog tipped peaks
Play peek-a-boo between the clouds,
smell of wet asphalt lingers on the air,

Lazy cows stroll
And graze on dew covered
hill hay,

While the old oaks
Sway in the cold misty breeze,
A rancher starts his tractor's melodic motor,

Like the start of ritual drums
That calls to the spirits
Echoes come.

On thistle thick and thin
Tawny turf braces
About the rocks that graces

Relief from
Bovine
And wind.

Dear, a deer,
Grace as it drinks with open ears,
As cautious eyes fight flight instinct of fright,

Squirrels dive and dart
While the cawing crows climb
to find a place in a tree like a freed kit.

As the sun slowly sets, a days close,
Turning the sky and clouds
Crimson, mandarin, and indigos,

Which finishes in a pale blue that
end in night
as grasses dance like a drunken knight.

GENERATIONAL MAZES AND MONSTERS

It's a generational gift
given by grandparents,
parents, aunts, uncles,
cousins, step-family

wanted or unwanted;

We wear it
like the handmade
ugly christmas sweater,
we so-un-wantingly were given,
but graciously garner

un-graciously we lament, wearing it

at every holiday, event, anniversary, or public outing,
we try to hide it under work, drugs,
smiles, music, conversations with friends

and/or avoidance.

When all we really want to do is pull
the little loose string to
unravel this itchy mess of
intertwined trauma,
to ball it up, to leave it somewhere

we'll forget;

but we need to use this intangible tangle to get out of our maze
built by:
parental violence, sibling passive aggressiveness,

shattered lamps and windows, broken doors,
overt drug abuse, rape, alcoholism, unknow family histories,
split up homes, death threats, unfinished dinners made cold
by arguments over money or lack thereof;

this labyrinth which is all at once
past, present, and future anguish.

The same maze that houses the Minotaur of PTSD
which is always on the search for us,
just as it looks for Theseus;

like Theseus we need to face our monsters and mazes,

stand to fight for our chance at escape,
slowly trace back with the un-crocheted tangles
of our diminished itchy sweater back to exit,
free of postulated twists and turns,
dangers and damages that lingered,

to step into the sweet air and warm light of growth,
freedom from itch, maze, and monstrosities;

Now ready to face the next challenge
that life brings forth from waiting gods
looking for more entertainment

of unknown ultimatums left unanswered.

A CHANCE AT IMPLEMENTING PEACE: IDEAS FROM OUR COMMUNITIES

If We were given the chance to implement peace
on the scale of
Community, State, or World

We would:

vote, spread positivity, attempt to understand
others points of view, you know, always getting along/kindness,
to look out for each other while caring,

not harm people
Or
the environment

We would:

try treating others the same way we want to be treated,
it's amazing how friendly attitudes and gestures
can change one's day and spread like wildfire,

create connections and build relationships with the different cogs
in our own little worlds,
to understand built culture and traumas we share or enjoy, while
we use affability to
integrate ideas and programs without the lack of love we so often
find amongst the observed

We would:

start small, gather together our communities to give back a piece
of

someone's life, make a change on that common ground we have to work, and
finish an explanation to a communal puzzler for the nation to view in awe

by doing this, WE rebuild trust amongst ourselves and our government, that has better
term limits, and implemented flat 10% tax. Our communities would know how to listen to understand, instead of listen to respond, then facilitate conversation amongst our peers

We would:

teach students how to and what empathy, love, respect is,
teach it to our children and our children's children
by insisting on peace in our own home

We would:

reflect considerations of care and calm actions
towards our species
while inspiring hope and a sense of ease

We would:

consider the lessons of religions, gods, their kingdom and promises of eternity, loosen the grip-gripe of money over our lives,
or to have a place of reconnection to nature,

but really that thing which We could do that would help the most to bring about peace:

get rid of all men.

NOSY LITTLE PIECE OF PEACE

When you smell,
vanilla, sweet scented candles, flora
in bloom, lavender, or Redwoods (high they zoom),

Does it bring you peace?

When you smell,
roses on fresh air, clean and crisp,
or early morning weather of Pacific Grove,

Does it bring you peace?

When you smell,
the creation of a season's change after a fresh rain, or
fried Friday bacon after daylight breaks when coffee has brewed,

Does it bring you peace?

When you smell
the ocean, or fresh cut flowerets,
when you glean the transition of fall or spring,

Does it bring you peace?

When you smell
cedar trees, the dried flowers of marijuana, laurel leaves in rain,
or fresh Chocolate chip cookies when baked (for me these are
hard to refrain),

Does it bring you peace?

When you smell
popcorn, a Bar-B-Que, the sweetness of cologne or perfume
from a lover, an Ex, a departed family member,

Does it bring you peace?
Do any of these smells let you have a moment
from the hectic chaos of the world,
what will allow you to allot a second to breathe,

to remember a part of life that was
happy, victorious? What waft that wavers will
bring you peace for a trice?

What smell brings you peace?
What smell allows you to traverse time
and transcend pain to pleasure, to be swallowed into quiet calm?

What smell sends you to a sanctuary of serenity,
What smell noses its way to part
a piece of peace amidst this place of imperfection?

What smell allows you to drop the trauma of life lived,
and live life,
what sniffed snuff non-mephitis musk allows you to remit,

what succulently saucy slanderous
smell slides through nose tip
to memory trip,

to thank the gods for what we get to experience
each day on this little ceramic ball that
swims and bobs in a celestial pool through the heavens?

What   smell   brings
          you   peace?

HOW PEACE FEELS TO US

Taking several deep breaths for a fullness of warm and refreshing
relaxed happiness
Taking several deep breaths for a fullness of warm and refreshing
relaxed happiness
No tightness in my muscles, solitude of no one calling my name,
floating on a cloud
No tightness in my muscles, solitude of no one calling my name,
floating on a cloud
And in my muscles no tightness a-calling-on, refreshing of re-
laxed warm floating happiness,
One-name-fullness for a several deep breaths of no taking my
cloud: solitude

Focus on positives, okay with negatives; of calmness, serenity,
bliss, anxiety free
Focus on positives, okay with negatives; of calmness, serenity,
bliss, anxiety free
Warm fuzzy feeling people with no friction or dreadful feeling,
unity
Warm fuzzy feeling people with no friction or dreadful feeling,
unity
Anxiety free bliss with serenity, feeling okay with positives or
negatives, unity on focus,
Dreadful warm feeling; fuzzy calmness of no friction people

Curled up animals next to me in weighted blanket of acceptance,
love, trust; safe environment
Curled up animals next to me in weighted blanket of acceptance,
love, trust; safe environment
Holding hands or hugs, sense of no apprehension, hot tub or feet
in sand, walk through nature

Holding hands or hugs, sense of no apprehension, hot tub or feet in sand, walk through nature
No sense of me next to curled up animals, love-trust acceptance of hot tub hugs, or holding feet in blanket, or hands in safe sand environment, nature-weighted walk through apprehension

Sense of fullness, focus on warm fuzzy feeling of positives, a no negatives environment, free blanket acceptance of hands holding bliss and serenity, my muscles floating in tub relaxed, a curled up cloud deep in nature, love hot safe trust hugs next, or no feet taking several animals, people with unity, warm refreshing calmness, or okay with solitude on sand, walk through
apprehension-friction of no one calling me dreadful, or feeling tightness in weighted breaths
For my name of no anxiety; happiness

www.ingramcontent.com/pod-product-compliance
Lightning Source LLC
Chambersburg PA
CBHW060627030426
42337CB00018B/3228